MW01232714

Bitcoin Investing

Guide To Blockchain And How To Mine Cryptocurrencies

Philip Salomon

Table of content

WHAT EXACTLY IS A BITCOIN, ANYWAY?

Bitcoin is a kind of digital currency that was introduced to the world for the first time in January of 2009. It follows the guidelines that were presented in a white paper that was produced by a person using the pseudonym Satoshi Nakamoto. At this time, the origin of the technology's development as well as the person or group of persons responsible for its creation are unknown. In contrast to currencies produced by governments, the management of bitcoin is handled by a decentralized authority. Because of this, the prospect of lower transaction fees that is connected with using Bitcoin is more tempting than the use of regular online payment methods.

Bitcoin is an example of a cryptocurrency that is currently in use. There is no such thing as a physical bitcoin; rather, balances are stored on a public ledger that everyone and everyone may view in complete transparency. This ledger is accessible to everyone. When utilizing bitcoin, each and every transaction must be verified, which requires an enormous amount of computing power. Bitcoins are neither generated or guaranteed by any banks or governments, and a single bitcoin has no value as a commodity on its own. This makes it difficult for bitcoins to compete with other forms of currency. On the other hand, there is a cap on the overall quantity of bitcoins. Despite the fact that it is not recognized as a form of legal payment, bitcoin has gained a lot of popularity recently. As a direct consequence of this, it has been responsible for the birth of hundreds of other cryptocurrencies, which are collectively referred to as alt-coins. The most common shorthand for "bitcoin" is "BTC," which stands for "bitcoin currency."

MAIN ELEMENTS

Bitcoin, the first cryptocurrency ever created, made its debut in 2009, and is today the digital asset with the biggest market capitalization.

In contrast to traditional forms of currency, Bitcoin is produced, circulated, traded, and kept afloat via the use of a distributed ledger system known as a blockchain. This system keeps track of all Bitcoin transactions. Satoshi Nakamoto was the one who first invented this technology.

In 2017, the digital currency known as Bitcoin hit an all-time high of about $20,000 per coin; but, only a few short years later, its trading price was less than half of what it had been. The history of bitcoin as a store of wealth has been defined by turmoil both historically and now.

Bitcoin was the first cryptocurrency to attain widespread recognition and success, and as a direct consequence of its achievements, it has been the impetus for the development of a great number of other virtual currencies.

ACQUIRING AN UNDERSTANDING OF BITCOIN

A network of computers (also known as "nodes" or "miners") is what makes up the Bitcoin system. These machines are responsible for running the Bitcoin code and storing the Bitcoin blockchain. The term "blockchain" refers to a digital ledger that records transactions using "blocks." Each block stores a collection of transactions in their entirety. No one is able to game the system in any way since all of the computers that are participating in the blockchain have access to the same list of blocks and transactions. Furthermore, everyone can plainly see that fresh blocks are being filled with new bitcoin transactions.

These transactions may be seen in real time by anybody, regardless of whether or not they run a bitcoin "node." An adversary would need to control 51 percent of the computer power that goes into a bitcoin for them to be able to carry out a malicious conduct. As of January 2021, Bitcoin has over 12,000 nodes, and this number is rising, which makes it very improbable that an assault of this kind would be successful.

However, should an attack occur, bitcoin miners—people who participate in the bitcoin network using their own computers—would likely fork to a new blockchain, thwarting the efforts of the attacker to carry out the attack. Bitcoin miners are people who use their own computers to participate in the bitcoin network.

The "keys" that are used to keep Bitcoin token balances may be either public or private. These "keys" are lengthy sequences of numbers and characters that are connected by the mathematical encryption process that was used to generate them. The public key, which is analogous to a bank account number, functions as the address that is broadcast to the whole globe and to which people may transfer bitcoins. This address can be found on the blockchain.

The private key, which is analogous to the personal identification number used at an ATM, is supposed to be a closely guarded secret and is the only thing that can be used to approve bitcoin transfers. Bitcoin keys are not to be confused with bitcoin wallets, which may either be physical or digital devices. Bitcoin wallets enable users to keep track of their coin ownership and simplify the buying and selling of bitcoins. Bitcoin keys are used to unlock bitcoin transactions. Because of the decentralized nature of bitcoin, it is never really held "in" a wallet; rather, it is stored in a distributed manner on a blockchain. The name "wallet" may thus be considered to be rather deceptive.

TECHNOLOGY BASED ON USER COLLABORATION

Bitcoin was one of the first digital currencies to leverage peer-to-peer technology to make fast payments, making it one of the earliest digital currencies overall. The autonomous individuals and businesses that own the governing computing power and participate in the bitcoin network are referred to as bitcoin "miners." Bitcoin miners are in charge of processing the transactions on the blockchain, and they are motivated by rewards (the release of new bitcoin) and transaction fees paid in bitcoin.

You might think of these miners as the decentralized authority that ensures the trustworthiness of the Bitcoin network. Miners get a predetermined reward for successfully mined bitcoin, which is then gradually reduced over time. The maximum number of bitcoin that may ever be mined is capped at 21 million. It is estimated that there are around 18,614,806 bitcoin in circulation as of the 30th of January, 2021, with just 2,385,193 bitcoin remaining to be mined.

In this regard, bitcoin and other cryptocurrencies work in a manner that is distinct from that of fiat money. In centralized banking systems, currency is issued at a pace that corresponds to the increase in the supply of products; the goal of this system is to keep prices stable. A decentralized system, like as bitcoin, determines the pace of release in advance and does it in accordance with an algorithm.

THE PROCESS OF MINING FOR BITCOINS

Mining is the process that is used to generate brand new bitcoins, which are subsequently put into circulation after being distributed by miners. In the majority of instances, mining requires the solution of puzzles that are computationally difficult in order to reveal a new block, which is then uploaded to the blockchain. This new block may then be mined.

The process of adding transaction records to the network and validating those records is referred to as "mine" for Bitcoin. Miners get a reward in the form of a fraction of a bitcoin for each block of cryptocurrency that they add to the blockchain. Each time there are 210,000 blocks, the reward is decreased by half. In 2009, the block reward was equivalent to fifty Bitcoins that had just been minted. The reward for discovering a block has been reduced from its prior level of 12.5 bitcoins to its current level of 6.25 bitcoins as a result of the third halving, which took place on May 11th, 2020.

The process of mining for bitcoins may be carried out using a broad variety of computers and other types of hardware. Despite this, the returns on some are much higher than the returns on others. Application- Specific Integrated Circuits, also known as ASICs, are a sort of computer chip, while Graphic Processing Units, also known as GPUs, are an example of a type of processing unit that is far more advanced. Each kind of chip has the potential to produce a greater return on investment. These intricate pieces of mining equipment are more commonly known by their colloquial name, mining rigs.

One bitcoin is divisible into 100 millionths of a bitcoin, which is known as a Satoshi. Each Satoshi is equal to one hundred millionth of a bitcoin. This indicates that there are eight decimal places available for use when referring to one bitcoin. In the future, if this becomes necessary and the participants in the Bitcoin mining process agree to the change, Bitcoin might be made divisible to an even higher number of decimal places than it is now capable of doing.

A QUICK OVERVIEW OF BITCOIN'S HISTORY

On October 31, 2018, the Bitcoin white paper was made public. This document provides an in-depth explanation of how the Bitcoin protocol operates and came as a direct response to the subprime mortgage crisis and the bankruptcy of Lehman Brothers. This publication shed light on the vulnerabilities that are present inside the existing financial system and provided an overview of such flaws. This new sort of currency trading is an upgrade over its predecessors, HashCash (1997), B-Money (1998), RPOW (2004), and Bitgold (2004), all of which were unsuccessful but gave useful insights. HashCash was introduced in 1997, B-Money in 1998, RPOW in 2004, and Bitgold in 2004. (2008).

In particular, Bitcoin mirrored the Cypherpunks, who were a group that fought for individuals' rights to privacy and who were aware, far in advance, of the challenges that the Internet would provide in terms of breaches to individuals' private. The Cypherpunks fought for individuals' rights to privacy and were aware of the challenges that the Internet would provide in terms of breaches to individuals' private. Satoshi Nakamoto was able to surround himself with members of this community who had already worked on the projects mentioned above, including as Nick Szabo, Hal Finney, Adam Back, and Wei Dai. This allowed Satoshi

Nakamoto to build a strong foundation for the cryptocurrency. The author of the work did so under this fictitious name (s).

Let us take a look back at the most important events that have taken place in the history of Bitcoin in the order in which they have taken place since the cryptocurrency was first created:

When Satoshi Nakamoto generates the first Bitcoin block on January 3, 2009, also known as the "genesis block," he formally launches the network. This event is generally referred to as the "genesis block." Following a period of nine days, transaction number one took place in block 170. It included the amount of ten bitcoins and was carried out by Satoshi Nakamoto and Hal Finney. Satoshi establishes that he did not mine a block earlier to January 3, 2009, by putting the phrase "The Times 03/Jan/2009 Chancellor on verge of second rescue for banks" in the block that is mined for the tale.

On October 5th, the inaugural exchange rate will be offered on the New Liberty Standard platform. This price, which is derived by assessing the cost of the electricity necessary to manufacture this quantity of bitcoins, has been established at 1309.03 BTC for each dollar as of right now.

On May 22, 2010, a programmer by the name of Lazslo Hanyecz successfully completed the first Bitcoin transaction that included the purchase of property. At the present pricing of the market, ten thousand bitcoins is equivalent to twenty dollars, thus the deal consisted of two pizzas for that amount.

The 17th of July marks the day when MtGox was born. This marketplace for trading cards will overtake all others to become the most significant destination for the trade of Bitcoin in the next four years.

On December 12, Satoshi Nakamoto turned up his duties as the project's leader to Gavin Anderson, a developer who is still working on Bitcoin to this day. This marked the end of Satoshi Nakamoto's tenure as the project's leader.

In February of 2011, Bitcoin's value reached a position where it was comparable to one dollar at that point in time.

Bitcoin is a form of payment that is accepted on the notorious dark web marketplace known as Silk Road, which has just reopened for operation.

The very first alternative cryptocurrency asset to appear on the market in direct opposition to Bitcoin. Namecoin and Litecoin were the first cryptocurrencies ever developed and introduced to the public when they first surfaced.

On September 27th, 2012, the Bitcoin Foundation was created with the mission of standardizing, preserving, and promoting Bitcoin.

On November 28, the first "Halving" will be place, which will cut in half the incentive that is granted to minors for each block of transactions. This will take effect immediately. The price as of this now is 25 BTC.

On October 2, 2013, the Silk Road was taken down completely. On November 7, the price of Bitcoin will surpass its previous record high of 237 euros, and on December 4, it will hit 912 euros, ushering in a new period of rapid inflation for the cryptocurrency's value.

Following the theft of 744,000 BTC in February of 2014, the largest marketplace in the world, MtGox, declares bankruptcy, which results in a dramatic decrease in the price of Bitcoin that will not be reversed until the year 2015.

The cost of the class drops from more than 750 euros to less than 160 euros within this time period.

On May 13, La Maison du Bitcoin became the first and only venue in France that is devoted to cryptocurrencies and other digital assets. Through the use of the Coinhouse platform, it is the organization's goal to fulfill its purpose of disseminating its knowledge and skills to the general public while simultaneously simplifying and streamlining the process of purchasing and selling cryptocurrencies.

2015

Several companies and organizations, such as UBS, IBM,

Orange, and the United States Army, are all working on use cases related to blockchain technology and bitcoin, both of which are beginning to be regarded more seriously by these companies and organizations.

The development of the Ethereum project, which will ultimately become the second most valuable cryptocurrency in terms of market value, is now under the leadership of Vitalik Buterin and is currently ongoing. Ethereum is a platform that does not rely on a central authority to run, and it enables the building of decentralized applications. Apps is the common abbreviation for these types of apps.

On August 2, 2016, the cryptocurrency exchange Bitfinex was the target of one of the greatest thefts in the history of Bitcoin, when 119 756 BTC were taken. This robbery was one of the largest in Bitcoin's history.

There has been a perceptible growth in the number of cryptocurrency projects, and the value of cryptoassets has been gradually and steadily increasing. Both of these trends are encouraging for the future of the industry. This is making a contribution to the ecology of cryptocurrencies in general as they continue to grow.

2017

On April 4th, Japan enacted a legal framework for "virtual currencies" and formally accepted them as a valid means of payment. This came about as a result of the country's recognition of their legitimacy as a medium of payment.

As a result of the development of cryptocurrency-related courses and the excitement around crypto assets, the price of a Bitcoin rose to over $20,000 in a short period of time. This digital gold rush has also shown the existing limits of technology as a worldwide method of payment by revealing that transaction costs may reach up to $30 per transaction. This limitation has shown that there is still a long way to go before technology can fully replace traditional payment methods.

On the other side, the Bitcoin community has shown its ingenuity and efficacy by coming up with solutions like as SegWit and the Lightning Network. Both of these solutions will greatly increase the capacity of the Bitcoin network.

2018

The year 2018 will be remembered as the year of the "bear market" in the minds of investors due to the enormous drop in value that Bitcoin experienced, which was equivalent to 85 percent of its all-time high.

The year 2018 is also being heralded as the beginning of the institutionalization of the market. This is due to the fact that regulated investment funds such as Greyscale are admitting a growing number of professional investors who are interested in acquiring exposure to Bitcoin.

2017 was a year of education for governments and

authorities, who spent the year teaching themselves about Bitcoin and Blockchain networks in general. This was a year of learning for governments and authorities. The events that transpired in 2017 are contributing to the formation of a collective consciousness in the year 2018, as well.

The Lightning Network was made available to the public for the very first time at the beginning of 2018, and since then, its scale has been consistently expanding.

2019 In 2019, the bear market will come to an end, and a major gain in the price of bitcoin will begin at the beginning of the year and continue throughout the year. This growth will continue for the whole year.

Bitcoin has achieved new heights both in terms of the amount of computer power that is committed to guaranteeing the currency's safety and the quantity of use that it is put to. Bitcoin has reached new heights in both of these categories.

WHO IS IN CHARGE OF BITCOIN?

Bitcoin was created by an unknown individual or group of individuals under the alias "Satoshi Nakamoto." These individuals have remained anonymous throughout the process. He (or she) has been effective in combining a variety of technologies, including as encryption and distributed registers, in order to build an efficient network that does not depend on trusted third parties. Satoshi's true identity has never been disclosed, and the developer stopped working on the project in 2011, despite the fact that his brainchild has had some measure of commercial success. Do you believe that, if Satoshi were to return tomorrow, he would be able to continue to exercise influence over Bitcoin? Is there a method that can determine whether or not the technique is risk-free?

People have been curious about the true identity of Satoshi Nakamoto since since the cryptocurrency Bitcoin was first introduced. This line of investigation has been looked into again and again on a few different occasions. It is not known why Satoshi Nakamoto made the decision to keep his name a secret; however, it is probable that he did so in order to avoid massive media attention and potentially legal processes, considering that Bitcoin is outlawed in a number of jurisdictions. Satoshi Nakamoto stepped away from the project in 2011, which transferred control of Bitcoin to its community of users. This brought to the realization of the dream of a decentralized and censorship-resistant network of value, which in turn led to the creation of a currency that is really one of a kind.

HOW CAN WE BE CERTAIN THAT SATOSHI NAKAMOTO IS NOT FINANCIALLY PROFITING FROM THE INNOVATION HE CREATED?

Bitcoin is software that is freely released under an open-source license, and users may see its whole source code on a website that is hosted on github. The examination of the program's source code allows for the precise characterization of the manner in which the program operates. Because of this, it is quite simple to establish beyond a reasonable doubt that Satoshi could under no circumstances control the Bitcoin protocol in such a way as to cause it to develop according to its own whims or to alter the composition of a particular portfolio. This is because it is quite simple to establish beyond a reasonable doubt that Satoshi could not control the Bitcoin protocol in such a way as to cause it to develop according to its own whim Because we believe that Bitcoin's underlying technology, which is both new and revolutionary, confers a number of advantages, we have made it possible for you to purchase bitcoins via our web platform. These advantages may be summarized as follows:

Who is responsible for maintaining control of the protocol?

There are many possible responses to this inquiry that one may provide. They are explained in this piece of writing by engineer Jameson Lopp in a way that is quite straightforward and specific.

Every aspect of Bitcoin was designed and implemented with the overarching objective of eliminating centralized control and single points of failure wherever and whenever they might be found. You are welcome to read our article regarding the limit of 21 million bitcoins, which is an important part of the protocol and can be found here. The article can be found here.

Even though anybody may contribute to the code on Github/bitcoin, a variety of safeguards have been put in place to ensure that the code and all of its following versions will continue to be secure.

PGP keys are the equivalent of Bitcoin private portfolio keys, and only a restricted set of individuals known as core developers are able to use them. PGP stands for Pretty Good Privacy. These essential developers have the ability to publish new versions of the protocol and digitally sign them using their personal encryption keys (PGP). As of this moment, there are five people who are in possession of verified keys. It is clearly acknowledged that the persons in issue have been significantly contributing to the creation of the protocol for a long amount of time, and this number is susceptible to change. The consensus of the group will serve as the basis for any decision on the admission of new members or the expulsion of existing ones.

Any other developer is allowed to offer proposals for improvements to the protocol, and it is the obligation of the core developers to examine those suggestions, assess them, and either accept or reject them as part of the protocol.

THEREFORE, THE PROTOCOL IS UNDER THE CONTROL OF THE DEVELOPERS, RIGHT?

To get things started, the Bitcoin software has been understood by a number of different individuals in a variety of various ways. There is no need to use Bitcoin Core, despite the fact that it is the main implementation that the majority of developers work on and that it is utilized by more than 95% of nodes. This is because there is no requirement to using Bitcoin Core. It is not necessary for the software to be extensible over the network; rather, it is required for it to be compatible with the protocol. This is comparable to the choices that users of browsers for the World Wide Web have, such as Chrome, Firefox, and Edge, to access the website they want to visit.

However, despite the fact that you are using a separate piece of software, it is still necessary for it to comply with the protocol. Having said that, the protocol is also within the jurisdiction of the core developers. It would be sufficient for some of them to agree to modify it in the way that they would want, therefore would it be feasible for us to continue talking about decentralization in light of this fact?

THE IDEA THAT ALL PARTIES SHOULD AGREE

Fortunately, not at all; the only responsibility that power core developers have is to make public and propose to the community new versions of the protocol. The ultimate responsibility for determining whether or not their computers should be updated to a new version rests with the individuals who control the network nodes. It is possible to deduce from this that the choice to alter the protocol is arrived at via a process of consensus among the individuals who control the nodes that make up the Blockchain.

There is no obstacle that would prohibit a new development team from forming and putting up a new version of the software. The consensus of the great majority of nodes is required for anything to be considered the canonical version.

This flexibility was used in 2017 for the purpose of the SegWit deployment. Miners were hesitant to embrace SegWit as the new protocol. Following this, a proposal known as

BIP148 was developed with the intention of additionally including node owners and soliciting their feedback. Due to the fact that this proposal was not included into Bitcoin Core, an implementation known as Bitcoin UASF sprang to prominence very rapidly. The amount of pressure that was applied by Bitcoin UASF was sufficient for the miners to incorporate SegWit using the procedures that are described in Bitcoin Core.

In a word, the technology and protocol that underpins Bitcoin's operation enables the cryptocurrency to grow in a manner that is both dynamic and governed by the concept of consensus, rather than the notion of unilateral choice. The answer to the question "Who controls Bitcoin?" is straightforward: "nobody and everyone at the same time." This is because the system that governs Bitcoin is not democratic, but rather based on agreement. You have entered the wonderful world of free software.

IS IT POSSIBLE TO HACK INTO BITCOIN?

A significant paradigm in Bitcoin is based on the cryptocurrency's apparent absolute security, which is supplied by its unchangeable and hack-proof blockchain. This security seems to be maintained by a decentralized ledger that cannot be altered. On the other side, we hear a lot about hackers in the Bitcoin industry, and every so often they steal hundreds of millions of dollars from those companies. What exactly is it like to go through the process?

WHAT DO YOU MEAN, HACKING?

Throughout 2018, there were a variety of assaults launched against Bitcoin and other crypto-assets. The beginning of the year was marred by a very unfortunate event, in which more than $500 million worth of NEM coins were stolen from a Japanese platform. Sadly, the lessons have not been learnt, as more than one billion dollars was stolen during the course of the year on a variety of platforms...

However, the hack of crypto-assets that has received the most media attention is unquestionably the one that occurred on the MtGox platform at the beginning of 2014. This hack, which involved a total of 700,000 bitcoins and made headlines when it reached the news in most countries in Europe and the United States, resulted in the loss of 700,000 bitcoins.

One thing that all of these assaults have in common is that they target primarily online sites on which investors deposit their cryptocurrency assets.

WHAT'S THE DIFFERENCE BETWEEN A PLATFORM AND A PORTFOLIO WHEN IT COMES TO INVESTING?

The phrase "storing Bitcoins," which we have previously explained, is not accurate in any way. The Blockchain is the sole place where bitcoins and other cryptocurrencies can be found. This holds true for all other cryptocurrencies as well. The owner of a bitcoin really only retains control of a private key. This key is used to validate transactions involving the particular bitcoin that the owner has.

When a person stores their bitcoins in a portfolio, like Coinomi or the Ledger Wallet, they have full control on their private keys and may spend their bitcoins anyway they like. Because of this, a prospective hacker will be required to access the private keys of the portfolio, which, depending on the portfolio selected, may be difficult or even impossible, for a result that is, at best, random.

Naturally, a platform that can be accessed online represents a far more lucrative target. Standard computer servers are used to facilitate the platforms' operations, despite the fact that everyday transactions involving bitcoins and other cryptocurrencies are worth millions of dollars. Investors often store their Bitcoins on one of these platforms, which means that the platforms themselves own the private keys necessary to spend the Bitcoins. If a hacker is able to get their hands on these private keys, they will instantly be able to retrieve all of the bitcoins that have been kept on the site. Another kind of attack involves manipulating the removal system of the platform in order to trick it into thinking that a valid cryptographic withdrawal has occurred, which allows the perpetrator to steal the cash belonging to several users.

HACKING OCCURS ON PLATFORMS, NOT ON THE BLOCKCHAIN ITSELF.

Hackers concentrate their efforts on the safety of online platforms, the software for which is often built by workers of the companies themselves. The software that specifies the Bitcoin protocol and the Blockchain, on the other hand, has only been proven to be flawed once, and that was in the year 2010. The error was immediately repaired, and there were no financial repercussions as a result of the problem.

One of the major factors that might explain the solidity of the protocol is the fact that it is open source, which means that anybody who wants it can read it. This makes it readable by everyone. It might appear to be a contradiction to open such a piece of software, but research and practice have shown that free software, such as the Linux operating system, is highly reliable and secure. This is because a large community works together on a daily basis to improve the software's quality and find solutions to any security issues that may arise.

Bitcoin is not an exception to this norm, and a community of over a hundred IT professionals is working on it every day to make it more secure and advance its functionality.

Therefore, it is incorrect to suggest that the many hacks that take place on internet trading platforms raise concerns about the safety of Bitcoin or the Blockchain. The actual protocol itself is not broken; the problem lies only in the software that is used on these systems. To provide a comparison, one might say that just because a bank is robbed does not suggest that the safety procedures for euro banknotes are flawed. This is because there is no direct correlation between the two events.

WHAT AFFECTS BITCOIN'S PRICE?

If a Bitcoin were a manufactured product owned by a company, the company that created it would be in a position to determine its price. This could be done directly by arbitrarily determining the price, or it could be done indirectly by limiting or increasing the quantity of Bitcoins that are available on the market. Because of the decentralized structure of Bitcoin, none of these approaches can be used to manipulate its price in any meaningful way.

The mining process results in a certain amount of newly created bitcoins over a predetermined amount of time, as we have seen in earlier sections of this article. Bitcoins are "distributed" to users in proportion to their share of the network's total computer power (hashrate).

Bitcoin, a volatile asset

The value of Bitcoin and other cryptocurrencies is prone to engaging in huge price swings on a daily basis. It is not unheard of to see rises or declines of 10% or more over the course of a single day, which is something that happens very seldom for other asset classes such as stocks or precious metals.

The value of Bitcoin, much like the value of these other assets, is decided by the supply and demand in various markets. At any point in time, various participants in the economy may choose to purchase or sell at a price that they find appealing. When a buyer and a seller are able to come to an agreement over a price, a transaction is completed, and the price is then determined in accordance with the most recent transaction.

Fundamental analysis

The evaluation of a project, including its technical and economic aspects, as well as the management of the project by the development team, are all good elements that may be used to determine the value of an asset like Bitcoin. We are able to add new ones, such as a large business that is now using the project technology and has the potential to grow its adoption. An important aspect that helps determine the value of an asset such as Bitcoin is a study of a project's technical and economic components.

However, due to the lack of clarity around the underlying asset, it is impossible to tell how much the cryptocurrency market is worth. The performance of the firm that is represented by a certain share may have a significant impact on that share's market value. Coinhouse provides you with a personalized program to invest in this market for a variety of reasons, one of which is this one.

Analyses of the technical nature

In technical analysis, the chart curves of different assets are analyzed in order to find patterns and forecast future developments based on historical market movements. This is done so that the analyst may make informed investment decisions.

Some cartesian minds would interpret this as meaning that it will rain on the next Wednesday as well since it has rained on each of the three Wednesdays before to this one. However, when the vast majority of economic players concur that the veracity of such signs, the market may in fact respond in the direction that was anticipated.

The purpose of "technical analysis" is to "detect patterns and anticipate future market developments by evaluating the chart curves of the different assets," according to one definition.

WHAT'S CRYPTOCURRENCY MINING? MINING CRYPTOCURRENCY

Even though cryptocurrency mining has only been around since 2009, when the first Bitcoin was mined, it has already caused quite a stir among miners, investors, and cybercriminals alike. Discover all you need to know about mining cryptocurrencies and how the process works here...

Mining cryptocurrencies, often known as "cryptomining," is a subject that is frequently discussed in internet discussion groups. You are undoubtedly familiar with Bitcoin, Dash, Ethereum, and other forms of cryptocurrencies from having watched movies or read articles on the subject. In addition, the issue of bitcoin mining is often discussed in the aforementioned pieces of information. But after reading all of this, you could be left with the question, "What exactly is Bitcoin mining?" or "What exactly is crypto mining?"

In a nutshell, bitcoin mining is a phrase that refers to the process of collecting cryptocurrency as a reward for work that you do. Mining is a term that refers to the process of accumulating cryptocurrency. (When referring to the mining of Bitcoins specifically, this process is referred to as Bitcoin mining.) However, why do anyone mine cryptocurrencies? For some of them, finding an additional source of money is a priority. For other people, it's about increasing their financial independence so they don't have to answer to the government or the banks. But regardless of the motivation, cryptocurrency is becoming an increasingly popular topic of discussion among computer enthusiasts, financial speculators, and online criminals.

WHAT'S CRYPTOCURRENCY MINING? EXPLAINING BITCOIN MINING

Obtaining cryptocurrencies via the use of computers to solve cryptographic equations and "mine" for them is what is meant by the phrase "crypto mining." Validating data blocks and adding transaction records to a public ledger, which is referred to as a blockchain, is the procedure that is involved in this process.

Mining cryptocurrencies is a transactional process that requires the use of computers and cryptographic methods to solve difficult problems and record data to a blockchain. In a more technical sense, mining cryptocurrencies is analogous to gold mining. There exist, in point of fact, vast networks of machines that are engaged in crypto-mining and that retain shared records through blockchains.

It is essential to have an understanding of the fact that the cryptocurrency market is in and of itself an alternative to the conventional banking system that is used on a worldwide scale. In order to have a better understanding of how crypto mining works, the first thing that you need to do is get familiar with the distinction between centralized and decentralized systems.

CONVENTIONAL FINANCIAL

Institutions are examples of centralized systems.

All financial dealings in traditional banking are managed by a single organization, which is also responsible for maintaining accurate records of these dealings and enforcing relevant regulations (ledger). This indicates that every single transaction must be handled via the centralized banking system, where it will be recorded and reviewed to ensure that it is accurate. In addition to this, it is a restricted system, which means that only a select few companies (banks) are authorized to interface to the centralized banking system directly. This is because it is a centralized banking system.

Systems That Are Not Centralized But Distributed Are Used By Cryptocurrencies

When working with cryptocurrencies, you won't have to deal with a central authority or a centralized ledger as you would with traditional currency. The reason for this is that cryptocurrencies operate on a decentralized network that makes use of a distributed ledger that is often referred to as blockchain (we will talk more about this momentarily). When compared to the traditional financial system, the "system" of cryptocurrencies enables anybody to instantly join to it and participate in its operations. This is in stark contrast to the traditional financial system. It is possible for you to send and receive payments without the involvement of a central bank in each transaction. As a consequence of this fact, it is often referred to as decentralized digital money.

However, in addition to not having a centralized management, Bitcoin also operates as a decentralized system. [Citation needed] This suggests that the record of all transactions, which is referred to as a ledger, be made available to the public and is maintained on a broad range of computers. This stands in stark contrast to the centralized banking systems that are used by traditional banks and which were covered earlier in this discussion.

To the contrary, in the absence of a centralized bank, how can transactions be validated to ensure they are not fraudulent before being recorded in the ledger? As contrast to a centralized banking system, which would verify things like whether or not the sender has sufficient cash to cover the cost of the payment, cryptocurrencies rely on cryptographic techniques to validate transactions. A centralized banking system would check things like this.

The miners who create new Bitcoins come into play at this point. The cryptographic calculations that need to be performed for each transaction represent a considerable amount of extra computational work that must be expended. Miners will use their own personal computers to do the required cryptographic work to add new transactions to the distributed ledger. This work will be done on the distributed ledger. As a sign of our gratitude and admiration for their work, they are given a tiny amount of the cryptocurrency as a reward.

CENTRALIZED, DECENTRALIZED, DISTRIBUTED

The distinctions between a centralized system and a decentralized one are shown with several instances in the picture that is located above.

An example of a centralized system may be seen in the section of the picture that is located to the left. The conventional, centralized monetary system that is used in the United States functions with the use of computers, networks, and other technology that are owned, managed, and kept up to date by financial institutions. Therefore, anytime you transfer money to a member of your family or a friend, the transaction is processed via the bank that you use.

a network of independently owned, managed, and maintained devices (which makes up the other half of the image) is used to make the graphic function. They contribute their assets to the development of this decentralized network and divide the tasks of concurrently validating transactions, updating, and maintaining redundant copies of the ledger.

IS IT LEGAL TO MINE CRYPTOCURRENCY?

In circumstances like this, the answer is almost always favorable. The mining of cryptocurrency can be done either legally or illegally, depending on a number of factors, the most important of which are your location geographically and whether or not you mine cryptocurrency using legal ways. Mining cryptocurrency can be done legally or illegally depending on a number of factors.

If, on the other hand, you mine cryptocurrencies using techniques that are outside the law, you are moving closer and closer to the domain of criminal enterprises. Because cryptocurrency mining is a process that demands a significant amount of computing power, this is the result. Some hackers, for example, would utilize Javascript in browsers or install malware on the devices of users who are ignorant of the risk in order to "hijack" the processing capability of a user's device. These users are oblivious of the potential risk. This particular kind of cyber attack is known as "crypto jacking," and there is a phrase for it. Be sure to keep a look out for a separate article that we intend to write and publish on this topic later on in this month.

However, it is crucial to bear in mind that governments all over the globe view the mining of cryptocurrencies in a number of different ways. This is something that must be kept in mind at all times. Mining for Bitcoin is seen as providing a service that is essential to the Bitcoin cryptocurrency system in some countries, such as Germany, according to a study that was released by the Library of Congress in the United States. This view was expressed in the context of the United States. The fact that Germany is one of such nations lends credence to the validity of this viewpoint. The LOC also reports that several local governments in China are cracking down on Bitcoin mining, which is leading many enterprises to stop mining Bitcoin completely. This is one of the reasons why the LOC is reporting this information.

In addition, the profits produced by mining cryptocurrencies may be liable to taxes in some countries, whilst in other countries, the results from such activities may not be considered taxable income. This distinction may exist depending on the country in question.

We'll go further into the aspects that give cryptocurrencies and cryptocurrency mining their irrefutable appeal in just a second. However, before we get into that, let's have a look at the mining process that is used to create cryptocurrencies. In order to do this, we are going to investigate the methods and technologies that are involved with it.

HOW TO USE CRYPTO-MINING

In a word, crypto miners ensure that the transactions they are working on are legitimate so that they may collect the benefits of their labor in the form of various cryptocurrencies. To have a better grasp on the more technical aspects of how most cryptocurrencies are mined, you must first get an understanding of the technology and procedures that underpin the practice. This involves having a solid grasp of what blockchain technology is and how it operates.

First and foremost, you should be aware that the idea of a blockchain revolves mostly on two components: mathematics and public key encryption. Even while I am a big admirer of the first, I have to be honest and say that the second isn't really my strong point. On the other hand, public key cryptography, also known as asymmetric encryption or public key encryption, and mathematics complement one another on blockchains in the same way as burgers and beer do.

Blockchain is the name of a decentralized public ledger that is used by traditional cryptocurrencies such as Bitcoin. The term "blockchain" refers to a collection of linked data blocks that each hold essential bits of information, such as cryptographic hashes. These blocks, which are an essential component of a blockchain, are collections of data transactions that are appended to the end of the ledger as they are processed. When individuals get to watch their transactions being added (chained) to the blockchain, it acts not just as an additional layer of transparency but also as an ego booster for them. This is because of the way the blockchain works. In spite of the fact that it does not include their names anywhere on it, many people nevertheless feel a feeling of pride and pleasure when they see it.

A Dissection of the Functions and Procedures Contained Within the Bitcoin Blockchain

The development of a blockchain calls for the participation of a number of essential tools and procedures at various stages. For the sake of this clarification, we are going to utilize Bitcoin as an example:

Nodes. These are the people and the machines that are a part of the blockchain (such as your computer and the computers of other cryptocurrency miners).

Miners are the individual nodes whose task it is to validate (also known as "solve") unconfirmed blocks on the blockchain by checking the hashes. This is done by mining cryptocurrency. Following the successful validation of a block by a miner, that block will be added to the blockchain. A reward in the form of a cryptocurrency is given to the first miner who notifies the other nodes in the network that they have successfully cracked the hash.

Transactions. A transaction is the item that gets this party began, or rather, it is the thing that sets the process of mining bitcoin rolling. A transaction, in its most basic form, is the act of exchanging one or more cryptocurrencies between two different parties. Each individual transaction is combined with those of others to make a list, which is then put to a block that has not yet been verified. The miner nodes are then required to perform verification on each data block.

Hashes. These cryptographic functions that only work in one direction are what enable nodes to validate the legality of bitcoin mining transactions. Every every block that makes up the blockchain has a hash as an essential component. A hash is produced by combining the header data from the prior block on the blockchain with a nonce. This generates the hash.

Nonces. In the language of cryptography, a number that is only ever used once is referred to as a nonce. The NIST defines a nonce as "a random or non-repeating value," which is essentially what it means. In the process of mining cryptocurrencies, the nonce is a number that is added to the hash of each block of the blockchain. This number is the one that miners are trying to solve for.

The algorithm of consensus. This is a technique inside blockchain that assists various nodes within a distributed network in reaching a consensus so that data may be verified. It is believed that "proof of work," often known as "PoW," is the first sort of consensus method.

Blocks. These are the separate parts that come together to form each blockchain in its entirety. Each block includes a list of all of the transactions that have been completed. Once they have been validated, changes to blocks are not permitted. When you make modifications to previously published blocks, it is necessary for the hash of the modified block, as well as the hashes of every block that has been added to the blockchain after the publication of the original block, to be validated by all of the other nodes in the peer-to-peer network. If this is not the case, the modifications will not be accepted. To put it another way, making changes to older blocks is almost difficult.

Blockchain. The blockchain itself is composed of a sequence of blocks that are recorded in the order in which they were created. This offers a degree of transparency due to the fact that blocks that have already been published cannot be edited or altered once they have been put to the blockchain. After all, everyone is privy to the financial dealings.

HOW CRYPTOCURRENCY IS MINED, STEP BY STEP

Now that we have that out of the way, let's get down to the nitty gritty of the process of mining cryptocurrencies so that we can have a better grasp on how it all works.

1. Nodes Confirm That Transactions Are Legitimate
Transactions are the foundation upon which a blockchain-based cryptocurrency system is constructed. So, in order to gain a better grasp on how everything fits together, let's look at the following example:

Let's imagine you're a crypto miner, and one of your other friends, Jake, lends $5,000 to your other buddy, Andy, so that Andy may purchase a brand new high-end gaming setup for himself. It is a top-of-the-line PC that has been outfitted with the most up-to-date gaming setup accessories available. (You know, everything from the LED keyboard and gaming mouse to the large multi-screen monitor and the top-of-the-line combination headset with a mic.) Andy decides to give him a portion of a Bitcoin unit as a form of repayment. Nevertheless, in order for the transaction to be finalized, it will need to go through the verification procedure (more on that shortly).

2. Individual Transactions Are Added to an Already Existing List of Transactions in Order to Create a Block

In the following stage of the crypto mining process, all of the transactions are compiled into a list, which is then appended to a fresh block of data that has not yet been verified. Continuing with the illustration of a transaction using a gaming system, the Bitcoin payment that Andy made to Jake would be considered an example of such a transaction.

By adding their transaction to the blockchain (after the verification process is complete), it prohibits "double spending" of any cryptocurrency by preserving a permanent public record. Blockchains are distributed ledgers that store information about transactions. The record is immutable, which means that it can never be changed or tampered with in any way.

3. A hash along with many other types of data are appended to the block that has not yet been validated.
When there are sufficient transactions added to the block, more information is also added to it. This additional information includes the header data and hash from the block in the chain that came before it, as well as a new hash for the block that is being added. The new hash is created by combining the header of the most recent block with a nonce, which is what occurs at this point in the process. This hash is

added to the block that has not yet been confirmed, and it will thereafter need to be validated by a miner node.

For the sake of argument, let's imagine that you have the good fortune to be the one who figures it out. You let the other miners on the network know that you've completed the task by sending out a message to confirm it and letting them know that they should check your work.

4. The miners check the hash of the block to make certain that the block is legitimate.

In this stage of the process, other miners around the network verify the hash of the unconfirmed block to determine whether or not it is legitimate.

But how difficult is it to crack a hash? Consider the following scenario as an illustration: using a SHA-256 hash calculator, you input the plain text phrase

"I adore cryptocurrency mining" and get a hash based on it. This implies that the phrase would become: "

8a0ab6e5058089f590f9872b3a299326ea36dfa13add8y0a141b 731580f558a7"

as a result of this. Now, I don't know about you, but there's no way in hell that I'm going to be able to understand or figure out what the heck that lengthy line of ciphertext nonsense means. It's just too much gibberish.

5. After the Block has Been Confirmed, it Will Be Published on the Blockchain.

On the cryptocurrency miner's side of things, today is the moment to celebrate as the proof of work (PoW) has now been successfully completed. The Proof of Work (PoW) is a time-consuming procedure that involves solving the hash and showing to others that you have legitimately done so in a form that they can verify.

From the perspective of the user, this essentially implies that the transaction in which Andy sent a portion of his Bitcoin to Jake has been validated and will be included in the blockchain as an integral part of the block. Naturally, since it is the block that contains the most recent confirmation, the new block will be added to the chain at the very end. This is due to the chronological structure of blockchain ledgers and the fact that new entries build upon those that have already been published.

HOW THESE PARTS OF THE BLOCKCHAIN ECOSYSTEM WORK TOGETHER

The question now is, how does this ledger prevent illegal changes and manipulations from occurring? The ledger's whole, including each and every transaction, is encrypted using public key cryptography. In order for the blocks to be acknowledged, they are required to make use of a hash that the miner nodes on the blockchain are able to use to validate that each block is authentic and has not been tampered with.

WHO (AND HOW OFTEN) DOES THE BLOCKCHAIN GET UPDATED?

Because there is no central regulatory body to govern or supervise exchanges, it is the responsibility of the computers that mine that particular form of cryptocurrency to maintain the ledger up to date. This is because there is no centralized regulatory authority. Additionally, there are regular changes made to the blockchain. As an example, Buybitcoinworldwide.com hypothesizes that the process of mining Bitcoin results in the addition of a new block to the blockchain every ten minutes.

Because the blockchain for cryptocurrencies is a public record, anybody may see it and contribute new transactions to it. To do this, you will need to use your computer to create random guesses in an effort to solve an equation that is presented by the blockchain system. Your transaction will be added to the next data block for review and authorization if it is successful. If not, you have to go fish and keep trying different methods until you either succeed at some point or give up. You might also choose to divert your attention and resources to anything else.

Let's take a few seconds to grasp the appeal of cryptocurrencies and why someone may want to mine them now that you have a basic understanding of what cryptocurrency mining is and how it operates.

WHEN IS THE OPTIMAL MOMENT TO INVEST IN DIGITAL CURRENCIES?

The quest for the Holy Grail by speculators has always been comparable to the hunt for the optimal purchase price of an investment that would guarantee the biggest return possible. The search of "cheaper" goods led to the missed opportunity to make numerous potentially successful investments. Speculators who attempted to sell their investments "at larger prices" often had a significant portion of their prospective earnings vanish as a result of their actions. Should techniques such as averaging the prices of several transactions be among the options under consideration?

Investing vs. trading

The reality of day trading is much different from the rosy picture painted by its proponents, who claim that it is possible to amass vast riches just by sitting in front of a computer for 24 hours straight. Forbes reports that 90 percent of day traders wind up losing money over the course of the year.

The majority of those who make up the remaining 10% are full-time traders who keep a close eye on market fundamentals and stock prices at all times. It is a challenging occupation that is also fraught with danger and calls for a high level of competence as well as the capacity to maintain composure in all circumstances.

Trading can hardly be considered a supplementary activity to another career, despite what many "training" merchants, YouTubers, and other online "influencers" may have you think.

There are only two ways to earn money: the first is via hard labor, and the other is by risking potential financial losses. Trading involves a significant amount of both labor and danger.

BITCOIN'S VOLATILITY AND FUNCTION AS A MEDIUM OF TRADE AND STORE OF VALUE

Bitcoin is consistently one of the assets that has the most severe price changes in a short amount of time, making it one of the most volatile investments.

When there is a high amount of volatility, there are more possibilities for traders to make money, but there are also more dangers associated with buying and holding the asset.

Investors face a greater degree of risk when dealing with an asset that has a high degree of volatility since the asset is more likely to experience significant price changes in a short amount of time.

Investors have the opportunity to increase their earnings (potentially) by taking advantage of assets that exhibit high levels of volatility.

The oil sector, commodities, and developing currencies are other highly volatile asset sectors. Cryptocurrency is also one of the most volatile asset classes.

The amount to which cryptocurrency investors engage in speculative behavior, the size of the market, the liquidity of the asset, the effect of news, and regulation, all have an impact on Bitcoin's price volatility.

The market for cryptocurrencies may continue its organic growth if governments take a pro-regulation stance and enterprises operating within the sector maintain an innovation-focused attitude. If this occurs, widespread acceptance of cryptocurrencies may become a possibility within the next few years.

WHAT IS IT TO BE VOLATILE?

Before we go into the intricacies of analyzing Bitcoin's volatility, let's begin with the fundamentals.

A statistical metric that indicates the dispersion of returns for a particular asset (such as Bitcoin, stocks, or bonds), or market index, is referred to as volatility (e.g., the S&P 500, NASDAQ 100).

Simply said, a greater degree of volatility indicates more price fluctuations (in either direction), while lower levels of volatility indicate more stable and predictable price levels for an asset. Volatility may be measured using the standard deviation.

When it comes to assessing the degree of risk that various assets provide for investors, volatility is one of the most significant aspects to consider. When an asset's volatility is great, the dangers that it presents to traders are also considerable.

It's always been one of the things that makes Bitcoin so appealing.

When we compared the behavior of Bitcoin to that of gold in one of our earlier articles, we discovered that whereas gold has an annual volatility rate of 10%, Bitcoin stands out with an astounding 95%. This led us to conclude that Bitcoin is the superior asset.

WHAT TYPES OF ASSETS ARE THE MOST VOLATILE?

According to the chart that was just shown, Bitcoin is one of the assets that has the greatest degree of volatility. This is something that can be seen above.

Even more noteworthy is the fact that Bitcoin (BTC), although having a high degree of volatility, has the lowest levels of volatility when compared to other digital assets. This makes Bitcoin (BTC) the least volatile of all digital assets.

Given that Bitcoin is the cryptocurrency with the biggest market capitalization, an infrastructure that is already well-established, a vibrant community, and a reputation that it has acquired as the world's first cryptocurrency, this makes perfect sense.

The energy industry, which includes assets such as oil, gas, coal, and technologies for renewable energy, is known for having the most unpredictable market circumstances among all of global finance. This is due to the fact that the energy sector encompasses assets such as these. Over the course of the last several years, the volatility of oil prices has even significantly outpaced that of Bitcoin. This trend is expected to continue.

When this post was published, the asset's volatility had

escalated to the point where it was 2.5 times more volatile than Bitcoin. This comparison is accurate as of the time the article was written. This was a direct result of the breakout of COVID-19 that is now going on as well as the oil price war that is going on between Russia and Saudi Arabia.

The commodity market is infamous for its high levels of volatility. The commodities market is comprised of natural resources such as oil and gas, precious metals, and agricultural things such as livestock and grain.

Emerging currencies are the national currencies of nations that are in the process of economic growth but have not yet reached their full potential.

There is a common practice of referring to the nations that dominate this sector as BRIC countries (Brazil, Russia, India, and China).

The degree of volatility that is associated with major fiat currencies is far lower than that which is associated with developing currencies (e.g., USD, EUR, GBP).

In point of fact, the asset classes that are the least volatile are low-volatility exchange-traded funds (ETFs), stocks of established companies operating in low-risk industries, major fiat currencies such as the United States Dollar and the Euro, low-yield treasury bonds of developed countries (such as the United Kingdom and Germany), and major fiat currencies such as the United States Dollar and the Euro.

HOW TO FIGURE OUT THE VOLATILITY OF BITCOIN?

The standard deviation between returns on the same market asset or index is the approach that is the most frequently acknowledged for determining volatility. Although there are other methods to evaluate volatility, this is the one that is most widely accepted.

You have the option of doing your own calculation of Bitcoin's volatility or making use of pre-calculated BTC volatility indexes obtained from third-party sites like BitPremier or Woobull.

Example Calculation

Consider for a moment that we are interested in gauging the degree to which Bitcoin's price fluctuates over a period of one year.

For the sake of simplicity, let's assume that Bitcoin's price at the end of the first month was $1,000, the price at the end of the second month was $2,000, and that its value continued to climb by $1,000 each month until the conclusion of the period.

Utilizing the standard deviation approach, the following procedures need to be taken in order to determine Bitcoin's volatility for this time period:

The first thing you need to do is determine if the price of Bitcoin is above or below its mean or average for the time. Adding up all of the values for each month and then dividing that sum by the total number of months is the simplest approach to do this task:

Consider the following: $1,000 plus $2,000 plus $3,000 plus... plus $12,000 is $78,000, which divided by 12 months equals $6,500.

The next step is to compute the disparity between the price at which bitcoins were last traded each month and the average price for the time period. Due to the fact that we need each data, we strongly advise utilizing a spreadsheet in order to compute this statistic (also called deviation).

Example: $12,000 − $6,500 = $5,500
It is necessary to square every deviation value in order to get rid of negative values.

Example: $(-5,500)2 = 30,250,000$
After you have obtained all of the deviation values for each month, you should put them together.

Example: 30,250,000 + 20,250,000 + ... + 30,250,000 = 143,000,000

To determine the variance, start by adding together all of the squared deviation numbers and then dividing that amount by the total number of months.

Example: 143,000,000 / 12 = 11,916,667

In order to get the standard deviation of Bitcoin's price over the course of a year, take the square root of the variance that you just determined.

Example: $\sqrt{11,916,667}$ = 3,452

The figure of $3,452 for the standard deviation illustrates how values are dispersed around the average price of one bitcoin. Make use of this value to get an understanding of how far the price of Bitcoin may diverge from the value of the digital asset on average.

Which Factors Have the Greatest Impact on Bitcoin's Volatility?

As was previously said, the bitcoin asset class is a very volatile one that is prone to huge price fluctuations in relatively short periods of time. Why is this the case?

A NEW TYPE OF ASSET CLASS TO WATCH

The cryptocurrency market is still in its infancy given that Bitcoin didn't even come into existence until 2009, making it one of the youngest markets.

And the lessons that history has taught us are that increased levels of volatility and instability are to be anticipated in a market that is still in its infancy and includes new technology. This is something that can be expected from a market that is still in its infancy.

Putting money into cutting-edge technology is a high-risk endeavor since there is a bigger possibility that the business will not be successful in its early phases.

The total market capitalization of the cryptocurrency market was very near to $204 billion as this article was being prepared.

To put this into perspective, the market value of Microsoft (MSFT) stocks alone is $1.32 trillion, which is almost 6.5 times bigger than the market capitalization of the whole digital asset business.

The gap between the market capitalization of the S&P 500 index (which is currently valued at $21.42 trillion) and that of the cryptocurrency sector is even wider, with the former reflecting a market cap that is 105 times larger than that of digital assets. The current value of the S&P 500 index is $21.42 trillion.

These figures illustrate beyond a reasonable doubt that the general population has not yet adopted digital assets in considerable quantities. [Citation needed]

However, as time goes on, we can anticipate that this technology will continue to advance, and investors in cryptocurrencies would argue that as more people come to adopt crypto for usage (as opposed to merely speculating about its value), we can anticipate that market cap will increase while volatility will decrease. This is something that investors in cryptocurrencies would argue.

DOT-COM STOCKS AND BUBBLE

Let's take a look at an example from the past of a very young industry that has seen significant levels of volatility.

The late 1990s and early 2000s are remembered for the meteoric ascent of internet-related technology businesses, which finally resulted in the Dot Com Crash, which is considered to be one of the greatest stock market bubbles.

According to research that was carried out a few years after the bursting of the dot-com bubble, the NASDAQ Composite index, which is comprised of many different tech firms, saw an abnormally high amount of volatility between the years 1998 and 2001.

During the height of the Dot Com Bubble, the NASDAQ 100 had a significant impact on the valuation of the NASDAQ Composite index, despite the fact that the NASDAQ Composite includes all of the equities that are listed on the exchange. In late 1998, the total market capitalization was dominated by technology stocks.

According to the figure that can be seen above, the level of volatility experienced by the NASDAQ Composite index was as high as 85% in 2001, when the collapse of the technology stock market occurred.

When the tech bubble finally burst, the NASDAQ Composite had such a high level of volatility relative to the S&P 500 that it had reached approximately 400% of the latter's level.

Many technology businesses went out of business as a direct result of the bursting of the dot-com bubble. Others had been able to make it through the stock market meltdown. Since that time, the technological industry has developed a respectable infrastructure for itself in addition to cultivating a positive reputation.

Because of this, the level of volatility experienced by tech stocks has dramatically lessened.

The volatility index (VXN) for the NASDAQ 100 has spent the majority of the time between 15 and 20%, and has never exceeded 50%, during the months of September 2009 and February 2020. (except in March 2020 due to the impact of the COVID-19 outbreak).

THE SPECULATION

Another aspect that adds to the price fluctuations and volatility of Bitcoin is the degree to which cryptocurrency dealers base their actions on speculation.

When traders actively watch the markets and rapidly move between assets in order to purchase the lows and sell the highs, potentially with the use of leverage, irrational market behavior may result. Because these traders do this without fully researching the facts or looking at the bigger context, irrational market behavior might occur. It is possible that this will lead to the use of leverage in certain scenarios. This is of particular importance for traders who keep a tight eye on the markets while at the same time using leverage in their trading tactics.

At a more fundamental level, if people hold a cryptocurrency, such as Bitcoin, only for speculative reasons – without any intention to use it as digital cash, or in the case of ETH as a means to develop decentralized applications, this can take away from liquidity (in extreme cases), but more importantly, such investors would be more likely to sell off their assets as soon as there is some negative news surrounding it, even if only because it is of no practical use to them. As a consequence of this, there is a chance that it may decrease. It is quite likely that this will have a detrimental influence on the current situation in terms of the actual use that is being made of it. This is something that has to be taken into consideration.

According to the findings of a study that was carried out by Chainalysis, just 1.3% of Bitcoin transactions were started by merchants during the first four months of 2019, while 3.9% were the result of peer-to-peer (P2P) activity of some other kind. Based on this information, it would seem that the principal use for Bitcoin is still the trade of speculative assets.

THE VOLATILITY OF BITCOIN IN THE FUTURE

Bitcoin is an asset that is known to have a significant degree of volatility, which is something that we are aware of. However, in your opinion, do you believe it will ever become more stable?

If the number of people utilizing cryptocurrencies continues to increase and the ecosystem around digital assets continues to expand organically, it is realistic to predict that this will happen.

If this occurs, the size of the cryptocurrency market may increase, which would bring new real-world use-cases for consumers as well as companies, while simultaneously resolving the challenges of speculation and liquidity that have plagued the digital asset economy. These challenges have plagued the digital asset economy for a number of years.

It's possible that a regulatory climate that's more friendly to cryptocurrencies may help bring price volatility down to more manageable levels. A setting like this would provide transparency, encourage confidence, and make it feasible for much more money to flow into the industry from the community that regulates it.

UNDERSTANDING THE DIFFERENT BITCOIN INVESTMENT METHODS

Bitcoin was created with the intention of one day functioning as a worldwide currency to replace those that are issued by governments. This was the original intention behind the creation of Bitcoin (also known as fiat currencies). Bitcoin, which was first introduced to the public in 2009, has since evolved into a highly volatile financial asset that can also be used to make purchases at retail locations and dining establishments that are compatible with the cryptocurrency.

It is possible for you to invest in Bitcoin; the question is, should you? You very definitely can, but the extent to which you do so will be contingent on how well you handle danger. You should educate yourself on the many various ways that you may invest in Bitcoin, the many different strategies that you can employ, as well as the dangers that are linked with this cryptocurrency.

INVESTING METHODS

During the course of the last ten years, several opportunities to invest in Bitcoin have been available. These opportunities include Bitcoin trusts and ETFs that are composed of firms associated to Bitcoin.

Purchasing Bitcoin Without an Exchange

The first approach to put money into Bitcoin is to use a trading software like Coinbase to buy a coin or a portion of a coin. You can also buy a coin using a fraction of a coin. To open an account, you will often be required to enter some personal information, after which you will be asked to deposit funds before you can begin purchasing bitcoins. When purchasing bitcoins via some services, a minimum deposit quantity could be required.

You will then have access to the performance of Bitcoin's price, just like you would with any stock or ETF, as well as the opportunity to purchase or sell Bitcoin. When you make a purchase, the details of that transaction are stored securely in an encrypted wallet, which you and only you can access.

THE BITCOIN INVESTMENT TRUST FROM GREYSCALE (GBTC)

Investors who are interested in putting their money into Bitcoin through the stock market may do so via Greyscale's Bitcoin Investment Trust (GBTC). Using Greyscale has a number of benefits that make an investment in bitcoin a more easily digested choice. To begin, shares of GBTC may be held in various individual retirement accounts (IRA), Roth IRAs, and other brokerage and investor accounts. This makes it simple for investors of all experience levels to have access to a diverse range of accounts.

An investment product that monitors the value of one tenth of a bitcoin is made available to investors. As an example, if the value of one Bitcoin is one thousand dollars, then the net asset value of one share of GBTC should be one hundred dollars. The underlying value is subject to a charge that is maintained by GBTC at a rate of 2%, and this fee has an impact on the value.

In point of fact, investors are forking out their money in exchange for convenience, safety, and liquidity (conversion to cash). GBTC makes it possible for investors who are less technically savvy to enter the bitcoin market in a secure manner by setting up robust offline storage methods.

The fact that GBTC also trades on the capital markets enables the company to transact at prices that are either above or below its net asset value (NAV).

TRANSFORMATIVE DATA SHARING ETF AMPLIFY (BLOK)

A mutual fund known as BLOK is one that is actively managed and has assets distributed among 15 distinct industries. The New York Stock Exchange's Arca market is where it is traded for trading purposes. The company invests in other companies that are involved in the blockchain industry and are working on creating technology that is linked to this sector. BLOK has a net expense ratio that works out to 0.70 percent of its total assets.

BITWISE 10 PRIVATE INDEX FUND.

The Bitwise 10 High Cap Crypto Index is a collection of big capacity currencies. The Bitwise 10 Private Index Fund, which attempts to offer security in addition to the simplicity of a traditional ETF, is based on the Bitwise 10 High Cap Crypto Index.

The minimum amount required to make an investment with The Bitwise 10 Private is $25,000. The fee rate for this service is 2.5%. In a manner similar to that of GBTC, the assets are held in cold storage (offline), therefore providing its investors with the necessary level of protection.

INVESTMENT TECHNIQUES

The community of people who invest in bitcoins uses the phrase "hodl," which is a deliberate misuse of the word "hold." Hodl has also become a backronym, which is when an acronym is constructed from an existing word. It means "hang on for dear life." "Hodling" refers to the practice of an investor keeping their Bitcoin holdings, often known as a "hodler."

Many people invest in Bitcoin simply by purchasing and holding the cryptocurrency. These are the individuals that have faith in Bitcoin's ability to thrive in the long run, and they see any volatility in the cryptocurrency's short-term price as being nothing more than a hiccup on its long road to great value.

Long Holdings of Bitcoin (Bitcoin)

The goal of some investors is to get a return more quickly by acquiring Bitcoin and then selling it when the price has reached its peak. It is possible to achieve this goal in a number of ways, one of which is to capitalize on the high rate of return offered by the volatility of the cryptocurrency in the event that the market moves in your favor. Additionally, there are now a number of bitcoin trading websites that provide leveraged trading. Leveraged trading is a kind of trading in which the trading website basically loans you money in the hopes of increasing your return.

Bitcoin Short Positions

During a Bitcoin bubble, it is probable that some investors may put bets that the value of Bitcoin will go down. This is very likely to occur (a rapid rise in prices followed by a rapid decrease in prices). Bitcoin investors first sell their holdings at a predetermined price, and then try to repurchase the cryptocurrency at a lower price.

For example, if you bought a bitcoin for $100 and then sold it for the same amount, you would want to wait until the value of that bitcoin decreased before purchasing another bitcoin. You would be able to make another purchase of that bitcoin at the lower price if the person who originally bought it subsequently changed their mind and decided they wanted to sell it. Your profit will equal the amount that the greater price you sell it for is higher than the lower price you acquired it for, and this difference will be where your profit comes from.

Finding a location that allows short selling might be difficult; however, the Chicago Mercantile Exchange (CME) is already offering alternate trading options for Bitcoin futures contracts.

There is always a chance that the market may move against

you, causing you to lose the money that you have invested as a direct consequence of this move. This is a risk that you take whenever you participate in financial markets. A trader of any sort has to have a thorough knowledge of the concepts of leverage and margin calls before they can proceed with a shorting strategy.

These changes may have a significant impact. When the value of Bitcoin shot up from roughly $40 to $140 in the span of only one month in April 2013, the whole globe watched in awe. That rise, on the other hand, was insignificant in compared to the boom that Bitcoin had in 2017. Bitcoin's price ranged between $900 and $1,000 at the beginning of the year. It surpassed $4,700 during the first week of September but then dropped to about $3,600 during the second week of the same month. Midway through the month of December, it reached an all-time high of $19,891.99, but less than two months later, it had dropped to roughly $6,330.

Glitches and hacks are possible on exchanges

Exchanges can be tricky because many of them have proven to be highly unreliable—especially in the early days of Bitcoin. One of the first and largest Bitcoin exchanges, Japan-based Mt. Gox, collapsed after being hacked—losing 850,000 bitcoins and hundreds of millions of dollars. In April 2016, a glitch in an exchange led to Bitcoin's price to momentarily drop to $0.60 on Coinbase.

The conclusion

The limitations of Bitcoin do not prevent its use. However, it is of the utmost significance that you are familiar with what you are doing and that you do not risk more money than you can afford to shed at any one time. Due to the fact that it is a highly high-risk investment, the proportion of your overall investment portfolio that should be allocated to it ought to be quite low.

You may choose from a number of different investment strategies if you are interested in Bitcoin. When you purchase bitcoins via an exchange, you expose yourself to the danger of price fluctuations. However, if you invest in crypto-tech businesses through a trust or an ETF, you may reduce the risk associated with purchasing coins.